I Like To Po You Will Too!

A House of #EdTech Guide to Podcasting

Dedication

To all the educators and learners out there who are looking to get started with podcasting, this book is for you. Thank you for taking the time to explore this exciting and engaging medium. Whether you're a seasoned pro or just starting out, I hope that this book helps you discover the joys of podcasting and inspires you to share your own stories and ideas with the world.

To my friends and colleagues in the #EdTech community, thank you for your support and inspiration. Your passion for using technology to enhance education is contagious, and I'm grateful to be a part of such a dynamic and supportive community.

Finally, a special dedication to my family who has supported me throughout this journey. Your encouragement and belief in me have meant everything, and I couldn't have done it without you. Thank you for always being there for me.

Chapter 1: Introduction to Podcasting

This chapter provides an overview of what a podcast is and its history. It also highlights the benefits of starting a podcast, including the ability to share your ideas and expertise with a broad audience, and the potential for monetization. The chapter serves as a foundation for the rest of the book, introducing readers to the concept of podcasting and its potential as a creative outlet and business venture.

What is a podcast?

A podcast is a digital audio or video file series that a user can download or stream to listen to. It's a form of media that's often used for entertainment, education, storytelling, news, and more. Podcasts can cover a wide range of topics, from business and education to comedy and true crime.

The term "podcast" is a portmanteau of "iPod" (a brand of media player) and "broadcast." Podcasts are typically episodic, allowing users to subscribe to the series and receive automatic updates when new episodes are released.

Listeners can consume podcasts on a variety of platforms and devices, including computers, tablets, and smartphones. There are numerous apps and platforms for podcast distribution, such as Apple Podcasts, Spotify, Google Podcasts, and more.

Podcasts are a popular form of media due to their convenience and versatility. They can be listened to in the car, at the gym, while cooking, or during any other activity, making them a flexible and accessible form of entertainment and information.

What is the history of podcasting?

Podcasting, a term coined in 2004 by journalist Ben Hammersley in The Guardian, has a relatively short but fascinating history. The technology that enabled podcasting began to emerge in the early 2000s with the adaptation of RSS (Really Simple Syndication) feeds, which were initially used to syndicate blog posts and news articles, to include enclosures or links to media files. This was the key innovation that made podcasting possible.

In 2003, Dave Winer, a software developer and one of the key contributors to the RSS format, and radio DJ Adam Curry, often referred to as the 'Podfather', are credited with developing the first podcasting services. Curry created a program called iPodder, which allowed him to automatically download Internet radio broadcasts to his iPod.

By the end of 2004, other podcasting tools had been developed, and the medium began to gain traction. In 2005, Apple added podcasting to its iTunes music software, significantly boosting the medium's popularity. This integration made it much easier for users to find and subscribe to podcasts. Consequently, by the end of the year, "podcast" was declared the word of the year by the New Oxford American Dictionary.

Between 2005 and 2010, podcasting continued to grow in popularity, with many traditional radio and television shows also offering podcast versions. The low cost of entry allowed anyone with a microphone and a computer to create and distribute a podcast, leading to a wide range of shows.

In 2014, podcasting had a breakout moment with the release of "Serial", a true crime podcast produced by the creators of "This American Life". "Serial" was downloaded millions of times and brought a new level of attention to the medium. Since then, podcasting has continued to grow, with major media companies, celebrities, and independent creators all producing a wide variety of shows.

What are the benefits of hosting a podcast?

Hosting a podcast can offer a range of benefits, both personal and professional. Here are some of the key advantages:

1. **Building an Audience:** Podcasts can help you reach a new and broader audience. They can be distributed globally and can attract listeners who might not otherwise engage with your content.

2. **Establishing Authority:** Hosting a podcast in your field can help establish you as an expert or thought leader. It provides a platform to share your knowledge and insights and to engage with other experts.

3. **Personal Development:** The process of hosting a podcast can help improve your communication and interviewing skills. It can also deepen your knowledge of your field as you research topics and engage with guests.

4. **Networking Opportunities:** Podcasts often involve interviewing guests, which can provide opportunities to connect with influential people in your field. This can lead to collaborations, partnerships, or other professional opportunities.

5. **Marketing and Promotion:** A podcast can be a powerful marketing tool. It can increase your visibility, drive traffic to your website, and help promote your products or services. It's also a way to provide valuable content to your audience, which can build loyalty and engagement.

6. **Monetization:** While it can take time to build an audience large enough for significant monetization, there are several ways to

generate income from a podcast, including sponsorships, advertising, crowdfunding, and selling related products or services.

7. **Flexibility and Creativity:** Podcasting is a flexible medium that allows for creative expression. You can choose the format, content, length, and style that best suits your message and audience.

8. **Personal Satisfaction:** Many podcast hosts find the process rewarding. It allows you to share your passion, engage with listeners, and potentially make a positive impact in your field or community.

Remember, successful podcasting requires commitment and effort. It involves planning, producing, promoting, and regularly creating content. But for many, the benefits outweigh the challenges.

Conclusion

Podcasting has indeed emerged as a popular and effective medium for disseminating audio content to a broad audience. This digital platform allows you to share your ideas, insights, and expertise with listeners around the globe, fostering a unique and meaningful connection with your audience. The intimate nature of podcasting, often consumed through headphones, creates a sense of personal connection between the host and the listener, making it a powerful tool for communication.

Creating a successful podcast, however, requires careful planning and execution. The first step is to develop a clear concept and format for your show. This involves identifying your target audience, deciding on the podcast's theme or topic, and determining the structure of your episodes. Whether it's a solo show, an interview format, or a narrative style, the format should align with your content and audience preferences.

Investing in good-quality recording equipment is crucial to ensure clear and professional-sounding audio. While it's possible to start with basic equipment, upgrading to higher-quality microphones and using a good pair of headphones can significantly improve your audio quality. Additionally, learning how to use audio editing software can help you remove unwanted sounds, adjust volume levels, and add music or sound effects to enhance your podcast's production value.

Speaking of music, it's important to be aware of music rights and copyright laws. Using copyrighted music without permission can lead to legal issues. Fortunately, there are many resources available for royalty-free music or you can commission original music for your podcast.

Promotion is another key aspect of podcasting. Leveraging social media, collaborating with other podcasters, and encouraging listener reviews can help increase your podcast's visibility and attract more listeners.

Finally, consistency is key in podcasting. Regularly releasing episodes helps retain your audience's interest and can lead to a more engaged and loyal listener base.

Whether your goal is to educate, entertain, inspire, or even to establish yourself as a thought leader in your field, podcasting can be a highly rewarding medium. It not only allows you to share your voice and ideas with the world but also provides an opportunity to learn, grow, and connect with a community of listeners. With careful planning, commitment, and passion, podcasting can be a powerful platform for achieving your communication goals.

Chapter 2: Choosing a Topic and Format for Your Podcast

This chapter covers the important first step of starting a podcast: choosing a topic and format. The chapter begins by discussing the importance of identifying your target audience and selecting a niche topic that will appeal to them. The chapter then covers different podcast formats, including solo, interview, and roundtable, and offers tips for choosing the best format for your podcast. The chapter also includes advice for developing a unique angle or hook for your podcast that will help it stand out in a crowded market. By the end of the chapter, readers will have a clear idea of the topic and format for their podcast and will be ready to move on to the planning and preparation stage.

How do you identify your target audience?

The first step in identifying your target audience is defining the purpose and content of your podcast. The central theme or topic of your podcast serves as a beacon, attracting listeners interested in that particular subject matter. For instance, a podcast focusing on entrepreneurship would naturally draw business owners, aspiring entrepreneurs, and business students. Therefore, a clear understanding of your podcast's purpose and content is the foundation for identifying your potential listeners.

Next, demographic factors such as age, gender, location, occupation, and education level should be considered. These demographic details can provide a broad overview of your potential audience. For example, a podcast discussing college life would likely resonate with students, while a podcast centered on retirement planning might appeal more to older adults.

Beyond demographics, psychographics, which encompass attitudes, interests, and behaviors, offer deeper insights into your ideal listener. Evaluating hobbies, preferred media, and personal values can help shape a more nuanced understanding of your audience. For instance, a podcast focusing on sustainable living might attract individuals who prioritize environmental conservation and are interested in eco-friendly practices.

Analyzing the competition is another effective strategy for audience identification. By examining other podcasts within your niche, you can gain insights into their listener base. Reviews and social media comments can provide valuable information about what these listeners are interested in and what they value in a podcast.

Based on the information gathered, creating listener personas, or fictional profiles of ideal listeners, can be beneficial. These personas can help visualize the audience and consider their needs and interests more concretely.

Finally, the process of identifying your target audience is not a one-time event but an ongoing process. Once the podcast is launched, data about the actual audience can be collected through podcast hosting platforms or audience surveys. This information can be used to adjust the content and marketing strategy as needed, ensuring that the podcast continues to resonate with its audience.

By understanding the podcast's purpose, considering demographic and psychographic factors, analyzing the competition, creating listener personas, and continuously adjusting based on audience feedback, podcast creators can ensure their content reaches and engages the right listeners.

Finding your niche

Once you have identified your target audience, you can select a niche topic that will appeal to them. This may require some research and brainstorming to come up with ideas that are specific, relevant, and interesting to your audience. You can also consider the current trends and interests within your audience's demographic, and look for gaps in the market that your podcast could fill. When selecting a niche topic, it's important to balance specificity with broad appeal, so that your topic is interesting and unique, but also accessible and relevant to your audience. Additionally, it's important to choose a topic that you are passionate about and knowledgeable about, as this will make your podcast more engaging and authentic.

What types of podcasts are there?

The beauty of podcasting lies in its diversity, catering to a wide array of interests and preferences. This essay aims to provide an overview of the various types of podcasts that populate this dynamic landscape.

One of the most popular types of podcasts is the "Interview" podcast. These shows typically feature a host who interviews different guests in each episode. The guests could range from celebrities and industry experts to ordinary people with extraordinary stories. Marc Maron's "WTF with Marc Maron" and Terry Gross's "Fresh Air" are prime examples of this genre.

"News and Politics" podcasts have also gained significant traction, providing listeners with in-depth analysis and commentary on current events and political issues. These podcasts, such as "The Daily" from The New York Times, offer an alternative to traditional news outlets, often providing more comprehensive coverage and diverse perspectives.

"True Crime" podcasts have seen a surge in popularity in recent years. These podcasts delve into real-life crime stories, often involving murder or other serious crimes. "Serial," a podcast that investigates a murder case over an entire season, is a notable example that has captivated millions of listeners worldwide.

"Education" podcasts are another prevalent genre. These podcasts aim to inform and educate listeners on a wide range of topics, from history and science to language learning and personal development. Podcasts like "Stuff You Should Know" and "TED Talks Daily" fall into this category.

"Storytelling" podcasts, which can be either fiction or non-fiction, are akin to audiobooks or radio dramas. They weave compelling narratives that keep listeners hooked. "The Moth," a podcast featuring real stories told live on stage, and "Welcome to Night Vale," a fictional series set in a strange desert town, exemplify this genre.

"Health and Wellness" podcasts offer advice and information on various aspects of health, from mental health and mindfulness to fitness and nutrition. "The Happiness Lab" and "Sleepy" are examples of podcasts in this genre.

Finally, "Comedy" podcasts aim to entertain and amuse, often featuring stand-up comedians, humorous discussions, or comedic storytelling. "Conan O'Brien Needs a Friend" is a popular podcast in this genre.

Podcasting is incredibly diverse, offering content to suit every interest, taste, and mood. Whether you're looking for in-depth knowledge, captivating stories, insightful interviews, or a good laugh, there's a podcast out there for you. The variety of podcast genres reflects the medium's adaptability and its capacity to cater to the unique preferences of its global audience.

Tips for selecting your format

Choosing the right format for your podcast is a critical decision that can significantly influence your show's success. The format not only shapes the structure and flow of your podcast but also sets the tone for your interaction with your audience. Here are some key considerations to guide you in selecting the most suitable podcast format for your show.

Align with Your Content: Your podcast format should align with your content and purpose. If you're sharing expert knowledge on a specific topic, a solo podcast might be suitable. If you're exploring diverse perspectives on various issues, an interview or panel discussion format might be more appropriate.

Consider Your Strengths: Reflect on your strengths as a host. If you're a great storyteller, a narrative format could showcase your skills. If you excel at engaging in conversations, an interview or co-hosted format might be a good fit.

Audience Expectations: Think about what your target audience would prefer. A younger audience might appreciate a more casual, conversational style, while a professional audience might prefer a more structured, informative format.

Resource Availability: Some formats require more resources than others. Interviews require finding and scheduling guests. Narrative podcasts often require significant scripting and editing. Ensure you have the time, resources, and skills to produce your chosen format consistently.

Experiment and Evolve: Don't be afraid to experiment with different formats in your initial episodes. You can evolve your format based on feedback from your audience and your comfort level as a host.

Consistency: Once you've chosen a format, try to be consistent. This helps set listener expectations and build a loyal audience.

Choosing a podcast format is a strategic decision that should be guided by your content, strengths, audience, and resources. Remember, there's no one-size-fits-all format. The best format for your podcast is the one that allows you to effectively share your message, engage your audience, and enjoy the process of podcasting.

Developing your hook and standing out

One piece of advice for developing a unique angle or hook for your podcast is to focus on a specific niche within your topic area. This will help you to stand out in a crowded market and provide your audience with content that is highly relevant and specialized. For example, if your podcast is about sports, you might focus on a particular team or league, or a specific aspect of sports culture. Additionally, you can try to find a unique perspective or approach to your topic that sets your podcast apart. For example, you might interview people who have a unique connection to your topic or use humor or storytelling to make your content more engaging. Finally, you can try to create a format or structure for your podcast that is different from what is commonly seen in the market, such as using a game show format or incorporating interactive elements. By thinking creatively and focusing on what makes your podcast unique, you can help it stand out in a crowded market.

Conclusion

Choosing a topic and format for your podcast is an important step in creating a successful and engaging audio experience for your audience. By considering your interests, expertise, and target audience, you can identify a topic and format that are well-suited to your goals and audience. There are many different formats and approaches to podcasting, including interviews, solo shows, panel discussions, and storytelling, and the right format for your podcast will depend on your content and audience. By carefully considering your topic and format, you can create a podcast that is unique, interesting, and engaging, and that helps you to connect with your audience in a meaningful way.

Key Points:

Identifying Target Audience: The chapter emphasizes the importance of understanding your target audience. This involves analyzing demographic and psychographic factors, studying competition, and creating listener personas. The process is ongoing and requires adjustments based on audience feedback and data collected post-launch.

Finding Your Niche: Once the target audience is identified, a niche topic appealing to this audience should be selected. The chosen topic should balance specificity with broad appeal, and ideally, it should be something the host is passionate about and knowledgeable about.

Types of Podcasts: The chapter provides an overview of various podcast genres, including Interview, News and Politics, True Crime, Education, Storytelling, Health and Wellness, and Comedy podcasts. Each genre caters to different audience interests and preferences.

Selecting Your Format: The podcast format should align with the content and purpose of the podcast, the host's strengths, audience expectations, and available resources. The chapter encourages experimenting with different formats and maintaining consistency once a format is chosen.

Developing Your Hook: To stand out in a crowded market, the podcast should have a unique angle or hook. This could be focusing on a specific niche within the topic area, finding a unique perspective or approach, or creating a unique format or structure for the podcast.

Chapter 3: Planning and Preparing for Your Podcast

This chapter covers the next steps in starting a podcast, including planning and preparing for your first episodes. The chapter begins by discussing the importance of developing a content plan and schedule and offers tips for creating a consistent and engaging flow of episodes. The chapter also covers choosing a name and branding for your podcast and offers advice for creating a professional and memorable image. The chapter then covers setting up recording equipment and software and offers tips for choosing the right tools for your podcast. By the end of this chapter, you will have a clear plan and all the necessary tools to start recording and editing your podcasts.

What is the importance of developing a content plan and schedule?

Developing a content plan and schedule is important for several reasons. First, it helps you to organize your ideas and create a structure for your podcast. By planning out the topics and segments for each episode, you can ensure that your content is well-rounded and flows smoothly. A content plan and schedule also help you to stay on track and avoid missing deadlines or running out of ideas. This is especially important if you are releasing episodes on a regular schedule, as it helps you to maintain consistency and keep your audience engaged. Additionally, a content plan and schedule can help you to set goals and measure your progress so that you can see how your podcast is evolving and growing over time. Overall, a content plan and schedule is a valuable tools for planning, organizing, and improving your podcast.

Tips for creating a consistent and engaging flow of episodes

1. Start each episode with an engaging introduction or hook that draws the listener in and sets the tone for the rest of the episode.

2. Use a consistent structure for each episode, such as starting with a brief overview of the topic, followed by interviews or segments, and ending with a conclusion or call to action.

3. Vary the content of each episode to keep things interesting, but maintain a consistent overall theme or focus for your podcast.

4. Use engaging storytelling techniques, such as using sound effects, music, or personal anecdotes to enhance the listening experience.

5. Engage with your audience through social media, email, or other channels, and incorporate their feedback and suggestions into future episodes.

6. Regularly review and assess the quality and engagement of your episodes, and make adjustments as needed to improve the flow and effectiveness of your podcast.

Overall, the key to creating a consistent and engaging flow of episodes is to plan ahead, be creative, and listen to your audience.

How do you choose a name and branding for your podcast?

Choosing a name for your podcast is an important step, as it will be the first thing that potential listeners see and hear. When selecting a name, it's important to consider your audience and the tone of your podcast. The name should be memorable and unique, but also reflective of the content and style of your podcast. It's also a good idea to choose a name that is easy to pronounce and spell, and that will be easy to search for online.

Once you have chosen a name for your podcast, you can begin to develop your brand. This involves creating a visual identity for your podcasts, such as a logo or artwork, and defining the tone and style that you will use in your podcast. Your brand should be consistent across all of your podcast's materials, such as your website, social media accounts, and episode artwork, and it should reflect the values and personality of your podcast. By developing a strong and consistent brand, you can create a professional image for your podcast and make it stand out in a crowded market.

Setting up recording equipment and software

To create a podcast, you will need some basic recording equipment and software. Here is a simple setup you can use to get started:

1. **A microphone:** A good quality microphone is an essential piece of equipment for recording a podcast. You can use a USB microphone, which plugs directly into your computer, or a traditional microphone that connects to your computer using an audio interface.

2. **An audio interface:** An audio interface allows you to connect your traditional microphone to your computer. It converts the analog audio signal from the microphone into a digital signal that your computer can understand.

3. **Recording software:** You will need recording software to capture the audio from your microphone and save it as a digital file. There are many different recording software options available, including Audacity (which is free) and Adobe Audition (which is paid).

4. **Headphones:** Headphones are important for monitoring the audio as you record. This will allow you to hear yourself clearly

and make any necessary adjustments to your microphone settings.

Once you have all of the equipment and software you need, you can start setting up your recording space. Choose a quiet, well-lit location with minimal background noise. Adjust the settings on your microphone and recording software to ensure that you are capturing high-quality audio.

Once you have everything set up, you can start recording your podcast. Make sure to speak clearly, enunciate your words, and take breaks if necessary. When you're finished recording, you can use your recording software to edit and enhance the audio, and then save the final version as a digital file.

That's it! With the right equipment and software, creating a podcast can be a fun and rewarding experience.

Conclusion

Planning and preparing for your podcast is an essential step in creating a successful and engaging audio experience for your audience. By developing a clear concept and format, identifying your target audience, and setting goals for your podcast, you can ensure that your content is well-suited to your audience and aligned with your objectives. Additionally, by researching and organizing your content, and considering factors such as music rights and recording equipment, you can create a solid foundation for your podcast and set yourself up for success. By following these steps, you can create a well-structured and professional podcast that resonates with your audience and helps you to achieve your goals.

Chapter 4: Recording and Editing Your Podcast

In this chapter, we will cover the basics of recording and editing your podcast. We will discuss the necessary equipment and software for recording, as well as tips for achieving high-quality audio. We will also go over the basics of editing your podcast, including cutting and splicing audio, adding music and sound effects, and exporting your finished episode. Whether you are a seasoned podcasting veteran or just starting out, this chapter will provide you with the knowledge and skills you need to create professional-sounding podcasts.

Tips for Recording a High-Quality Podcast

To record a high-quality podcast, you will need to invest in good-quality recording equipment and find a quiet, distraction-free space to record in. It's also important to use a pop filter to reduce plosives and wear headphones while recording to monitor your audio. Additionally, you should test your equipment and recording space before you start, take breaks as needed, and consider editing your podcast after recording to remove any mistakes or background noise. By following these steps, you can ensure that your podcast is recorded at the highest possible quality.

Here are some tips for recording a high-quality podcast:

1. Invest in a good quality microphone and recording equipment. This will ensure that your audio is clear and free of background noise.

2. Choose a quiet and distraction-free recording space. This will help to minimize background noise and ensure that you can focus on recording your podcast.

3. Use a pop filter to reduce plosives, which are the popping sounds that can occur when you say words with plosive consonants (like "p" or "b"). A pop filter can help to improve the overall quality of your audio.

4. Use headphones while recording to monitor your audio and ensure that you are speaking at a consistent volume. This will also help you to catch any mistakes or errors as they happen.

5. Test your equipment and recording space before you start recording. This will give you a chance to make any necessary adjustments and ensure that everything is working properly.

6. Take breaks as needed and don't be afraid to stop and redo a section if you need to. It's better to take the time to get it right than to rush and end up with a subpar recording.

7. Consider editing your podcast after recording to remove any mistakes or background noise. This can help to improve the overall quality of your podcast and make it more enjoyable for your listeners.

Where should I record my podcast?

There are many great places to record a podcast, and the best location will depend on your specific needs and preferences. Some factors to consider when choosing a location to record your podcast include the acoustics of the space, the availability of recording equipment, and the accessibility of the location.

Here are some great places to record a podcast:

- **A dedicated recording studio:** If you have the budget, renting a dedicated recording studio can be an excellent option. Recording studios are designed specifically for recording audio, so they often have good acoustics and are equipped with high-quality recording equipment.

- **A quiet room in your home:** If you don't want to rent a recording studio, you can create a studio-like environment in a quiet room in your home. Make sure the room has good acoustics and isn't near a busy street or other noisy areas.
- **Co-working space or library:** Co-working spaces and libraries are often quiet and have good acoustics, making them great places to record a podcast. Some co-working spaces and libraries even have recording equipment that you can use.
- **A coffee shop or cafe:** Coffee shops and cafes can be good places to record a podcast if you don't mind a little background noise. The ambient noise can add some character to your podcast, but make sure it's not too loud.

Basic Podcast Editing Techniques

It's important to edit your podcast because it can help to improve the overall quality and clarity of your audio. Editing allows you to remove any mistakes, background noise, or other unwanted elements from your recording, which can make your podcast more enjoyable for your listeners. Additionally, editing can help you to fine-tune the overall structure and flow of your podcast, and make it more engaging and cohesive. By taking the time to edit your podcast, you can ensure that it is professional and polished and that it effectively conveys your message to your audience.

Here are some basic podcast editing techniques:

1. **Trimming:** This involves cutting out any unnecessary or unwanted sections of audio from your recording. This can include things like long pauses, stuttering, or mistakes.

2. **Splitting:** This involves dividing your audio into separate segments or tracks, which can make it easier to edit and mix your podcast.

3. **Fading:** This involves gradually increasing or decreasing the volume of your audio over a set period of time. This can be used to smooth transitions between segments or to add emphasis to a particular part of your podcast.

4. **Normalization:** This involves adjusting the overall volume of your audio to ensure that it is consistent throughout your podcast. This can help to make your podcast more pleasant to listen to and avoid any sudden loud or quiet moments.

5. **Equalization:** This involves adjusting the balance of different frequencies in your audio to improve the overall sound quality. This can help to make your podcast more clear and intelligible.

6. **Compression:** This involves reducing the dynamic range of your audio, which can help to make quieter sounds louder and louder sounds quieter. This can help to make your podcast more consistent and easy to listen to.

By using these editing techniques, you can improve the overall quality and clarity of your podcast.

Recommended YouTube Viewing:

- [Audacity Podcast Tutorial - QUICKLY Edit a Podcast and Sound Great!](#) (Music Radio Creative)

- [How To Edit A Podcast For Free On Mac || GarageBand Tutorial](#) (Riverside.fm)

Music in Your Podcast

When looking to add music to a podcast, there are a few things to consider. First, you should make sure that you have the appropriate rights and licenses to use the music in your podcast. This may involve obtaining permission from the composer, artist, or music publisher, and paying any necessary fees. Second, you should consider the overall tone and style of the music and how it will fit with your podcast. The music should complement your content and not distract from it. Finally, you should think about the placement of the music within your podcast and how it will affect the pacing and flow of your content. By carefully considering these factors, you can effectively use music to enhance your podcast.

Here are some Dos and Don'ts when it comes to adding music to a podcast:

Do:
- Make sure you have the appropriate rights and licenses to use the music in your podcast
- Choose music that fits the tone and style of your podcast
- Use the music to enhance your content and not distract from it
- Consider the placement of the music within your podcast and how it will affect the pacing and flow of your content

Don't:
- Use copyrighted music without permission
- Choose music that is too loud or overbearing
- Use music to cover up poor-quality audio or other mistakes in your recording
- Let the music dominate your podcast and drown out your voice or other important audio elements.

What is Podsafe Audio?

Podsafe audio refers to audio that is specifically licensed for use in podcasts. This means that the creator of the audio has given permission for it to be used in podcasts and that any necessary fees or royalties have been paid. Podsafe audio is often created specifically for podcasts and may be available for free or for a fee from online repositories or websites that specialize in Podsafe audio. By using Podsafe audio, podcasters can ensure that they are using music, sound effects, and other audio elements legally and without infringing on anyone's rights.

There are several sources of royalty-free and Creative Commons-licensed music that are popular among podcasters. Some of the best options include:

- **Free Music Archive (FMA):** FMA is a website that offers a wide variety of royalty-free music that you can use in your podcast as long as you give credit to the artist. The music on FMA is curated by a team of experts, so you can be sure that you're getting high-quality tracks.
- **Incompetech:** Incompetech is another website that offers a large selection of royalty-free music. The music on this website is composed by Kevin MacLeod, and it covers a wide range of genres and moods.
- **Jamendo:** Jamendo is a website that offers a large selection of Creative Commons-licensed music. The music on this website is licensed under various Creative Commons licenses, so you'll need to check the terms of the license for each track to see how you can use it.

Conclusion

Recording and editing your podcast are crucial steps in creating a high-quality and engaging audio experience for your listeners. By investing in good quality recording equipment, finding a quiet and distraction-free space to record in, and using techniques such as trimming, splitting, fading, normalization, equalization, and compression, you can ensure that your podcast is polished and professional. Additionally, by considering factors such as music rights and placement, you can effectively use music and other audio elements to enhance your podcast. By following these steps, you can create a podcast that is engaging, well-structured, and enjoyable for your audience.

Key Points:

Tips for Recording a High-Quality Podcast: Invest in good-quality recording equipment, choose a quiet recording space, use a pop filter and headphones, test your equipment and space, take breaks and redo sections if needed, and consider editing your podcast after recording. Following these steps ensures a podcast recorded at the highest possible quality.

Basic Podcast Editing Techniques: Utilize trimming to remove unnecessary sections, splitting for easier editing, fading for smooth transitions, normalization for consistent volume, equalization for improved sound quality, and compression for a balanced audio experience. Editing enhances the overall quality and clarity of your podcast.

Adding Music to Your Podcast: Obtain appropriate rights and licenses for music, choose music that complements your podcast's tone and style, use it to enhance your content without overpowering, and consider its placement and impact on pacing. Thoughtful inclusion of music can elevate your podcast's appeal.

Chapter 5: Hosting, Promoting, & Distributing Your Podcast

In today's digital age, podcasts have become a popular medium for sharing ideas and information. With the rise of streaming platforms, it has become easier than ever to create and distribute a podcast. However, simply creating a podcast is not enough - you also need to promote and distribute it in order to reach a wider audience. In this chapter, we will discuss the various strategies and techniques that you can use to promote and distribute your podcast. We will also discuss the importance of building an online presence and engaging with your audience. By following the advice in this chapter, you can increase the visibility of your podcast and reach more listeners.

What is a podcast media host?

A podcast media host is a service that provides storage and distribution for podcast audio files. When you create a podcast, you will need to record and edit your audio files, and then upload them to a media host. The media host will then make your audio files available for download or streaming on various platforms, such as Apple Podcasts or Spotify. In addition to hosting your audio files, a podcast media host may also provide additional features, such as website hosting for your podcast's website, statistics about your podcast's performance, and tools for managing your podcast's RSS feed.

Some of the most popular podcast media hosting companies include:

- Anchor
- Blubrry
- Buzzsprout
- Captivate
- Castos
- Fireside
- Libsyn (use promo code NESI)
- Podbean
- Simplecast
- Spreaker
- Transistor

These companies offer a range of hosting plans and pricing options, and some also offer additional features such as website hosting, analytics, and support for integrations with other tools and platforms. It's important to research and compare the features and pricing of different podcast media hosting companies before choosing one that is right for your podcast.

Submitting your podcast to popular directories (Apple, Spotify, Google, etc.)

A podcast directory is a website or platform that allows users to search for and discover podcasts. These directories typically include a list of podcasts organized by category or genre, along with descriptions and other information about each podcast. Some examples of popular podcast directories include Apple Podcasts, Spotify, and Google Podcasts. Podcast directories make it easier for listeners to find and access podcasts on a variety of different platforms. Some directories also offer additional features, such as the ability to subscribe to podcasts or leave reviews.

How to submit your podcast to a podcast directory?

The process for submitting a podcast to a directory will vary depending on the specific directory you are using. In general, however, the steps for submitting a podcast to a directory are as follows:

1. Create an account on the podcast directory's website. This will typically require providing your name, email address, and other basic information.

2. Once you have created an account, you will need to provide the URL (web address) of your podcast's RSS feed. Your RSS feed is essentially a feed of information about your podcast, including the title, description, episode titles, and other metadata. If you are not sure where to find your podcast's RSS feed, you can typically find it on your podcast hosting platform.

3. After you have provided the URL of your podcast's RSS feed, the directory will typically verify the feed to make sure it is valid and properly formatted. This process may take a few days.

4. Once your podcast's feed has been verified, it will be added to the directory's list of podcasts. This will typically take a few more days.

5. Once your podcast has been added to the directory, you can typically update your podcast's information, such as the title, description, and episode titles, through the directory's website. You can also use the directory's website to view statistics about your podcast, such as the number of downloads and the number of subscribers.

Promoting Your Podcast

Promoting your podcast on social media and other online platforms requires strategic thinking. Let's explore some effective strategies:

1. **Share updates and new episodes of your podcast on social media.** This builds anticipation and excitement among your followers while attracting new listeners. Additionally, engage with your audience by responding to comments, questions, and sharing extra content related to your podcast.

2. **Collaborate with other podcasters or influencers in your niche.** By guesting on other podcasts or partnering with influencers, you can introduce your podcast to a new audience and potentially gain more listeners.

3. **Increase the visibility of your podcast on social media by leveraging hashtags.** Use relevant hashtags in your posts to make it easier for people to discover your podcast and join the conversation.

4. **Utilize the unique features of different social media platforms to promote your podcast creatively.** For example, share behind-the-scenes footage of your podcast recording process on Instagram Stories or use LinkedIn to share articles and written content related to your podcast's topic.

5. **Consider utilizing paid advertising on social media platforms like Facebook and Instagram.** Running targeted ads can help you reach a larger audience and attract more listeners.

6. **To succeed, consistency, engagement, and creativity are essential.** Regularly share updates, engage with your audience, and establish a strong online presence for your podcast.

Now, let's explore some popular and effective social media platforms for promoting your podcast:

- **Twitter:** This platform enables real-time updates and audience engagement. Share links to new episodes and respond to comments and questions from listeners.

- **Threads:** This platform is similar to Twitter and is one of the fastest growing apps of 2023.

- **Facebook:** Reach a large audience through this powerful platform. Share updates about your podcast and run targeted ads to reach new listeners.

- **Instagram:** Leverage Instagram's visual appeal to share behind-the-scenes footage and engaging content related to your podcast. Running ads can also help you reach a broader audience.

- **LinkedIn:** Connect with professionals and influencers in your niche on this professional networking platform. Share written content and articles related to your podcast's topic.

Remember, the choice of the best social media platform for promoting your podcast depends on your specific goals and audience. Consider the unique features and demographics of each platform to decide where to focus your efforts.

Building an email list

There are several reasons why a podcaster should build an email list.

An email list gives you direct access to your audience. By collecting email addresses from your listeners, you can send them updates and announcements about your podcast, as well as special offers or other content. This can help to foster a sense of community among your listeners and keep them engaged with your podcast.

An email list allows you to reach your audience even if they are not actively listening to your podcast. For example, if someone subscribes to your email list but then stops listening to your podcast, you can still send them updates and reminders about your show. This can help to keep your podcast top-of-mind for your audience and prevent them from losing interest.

An email list can help you to grow your audience. By offering a compelling incentive, such as a discount or exclusive content, to encourage people to join your email list, you can attract new listeners to your podcast. You can then use your email list to keep these listeners engaged and encourage them to become regular listeners of your podcast.

Some examples of popular email list-building companies include:

- AWeber
- ActiveCampaign
- Campaign Monitor
- Constant Contact
- ConvertKit
- Drip
- GetResponse
- HubSpot
- Mailchimp
- MailerLite

These companies offer a range of features and pricing options, and some also offer additional tools and services for managing and growing your email list. It's important to research and compare the features and pricing of different email list-building companies before choosing one that is right for your podcast.

Building an email list is an important part of promoting and growing your podcast. By collecting email addresses from your listeners, you can stay connected with them and keep them engaged with your content.

Conclusion

It almost doesn't need to be said but, hosting, promoting, and distributing your podcast are essential steps in creating a successful podcast. By choosing a reliable and feature-rich media host, and utilizing strategies such as social media marketing and email list building, you can increase the visibility and reach of your podcast and attract more listeners. In addition, by building and engaging with an online community of fans and followers, you can foster a sense of community and keep your audience engaged with your content. By following the advice in this chapter, you can take your podcast to the next level and reach a wider audience.

Key Points:

Choose a reliable podcast media host: When selecting a podcast media host, pick a service that can store and distribute your podcast audio files effectively. Look for companies like Anchor, Blubrry, or Podbean that offer features such as storage, website hosting, and performance statistics for your podcast. Research and compare their plans and pricing options to find the right fit for your podcast's needs.

Submit your podcast to popular directories: Make sure to submit your podcast to well-known directories like Apple Podcasts, Spotify, and Google Podcasts. These directories allow listeners to easily find and access your podcast. Create an account on the directory's website, provide your podcast's RSS feed URL (which can be found on your podcast hosting platform), and wait for verification and inclusion in the directory. This process ensures that your podcast reaches a wider audience and increases its visibility.

Promote your podcast through social media marketing: Utilize social media platforms like Twitter, Facebook, Instagram, and LinkedIn to promote your podcast effectively. Share updates and new episodes, engage with your audience by responding to comments and questions, collaborate with other podcasters or influencers in your niche, and use relevant hashtags to reach a broader audience. Take advantage of each platform's unique features, such as sharing behind-the-scenes footage on Instagram Stories or sharing written content on LinkedIn. Consistency, engagement, and creativity are essential in building an online presence for your podcast and attracting more listeners.

Chapter 6: Monetizing Your Podcast

In today's digital age, podcasts have become a popular medium for sharing ideas, stories, and information. As a result, many podcasters are looking for ways to turn their passion into a profitable venture. In this chapter, we will explore some of the most effective ways to monetize your podcast, including advertising, sponsorships, and selling merchandise. We will also discuss the importance of building a loyal audience and creating high-quality content in order to maximize your income potential. By the end of this chapter, you will have a better understanding of how to monetize your podcast and take the first steps toward financial success.

Do you need to monetize your podcast?

Whether or not you need to monetize your podcast will depend on your individual goals and circumstances. If you are creating a podcast as a hobby and are not interested in generating income from it, then you may not need to monetize your show. On the other hand, if you are looking to make a living from your podcast or use it as a way to promote your business, then monetizing your show will likely be an important part of achieving your goals.

Why should you consider monetizing your podcast?

Whether or not you need to monetize your podcast will depend on your individual goals and circumstances. If you are looking to make a living from your podcast or use it as a way to promote your business, then monetizing your show will likely be an important part of achieving your goals.

There are several reasons why you may want to consider monetizing your podcast, including making a living, supporting your business, creating high-quality content, and building a loyal audience. Monetizing your podcast can provide you with the resources and financial support to invest in your show and turn your passion into a profitable venture.

Strategies for monetizing your podcast

There are several different ways to monetize a podcast, including:

1. **Advertising:** One of the most common ways to monetize a podcast is by selling advertising space. You can either sell ads directly to advertisers or use an advertising network to help you find and place ads.

2. **Sponsorships:** Another way to monetize your podcast is by securing sponsorships from companies or organizations that are interested in reaching your audience. Sponsorships typically involve a company paying you to mention their product or service on your show.

3. **Crowdfunding:** Crowdfunding is a way that allows listeners to support their favorite creators by making recurring payments (known as pledges). Podcasters can use a platform like Patreon to offer exclusive content or perks to their supporters in exchange for their support.

4. **Merchandise:** If you have a loyal and engaged audience, you can sell merchandise such as t-shirts, stickers, or other branded items to generate income.

5. **Courses and workshops:** If you have expertise in a particular subject, you can create and sell online courses or workshops to your audience.

6. **Consulting and coaching:** If you have a successful podcast, you may be able to leverage your expertise to offer consulting or coaching services to others in your field.

It's important to note that the best way to monetize your podcast will depend on your specific audience and the content of your show. It may take some experimentation to find the right approach for your particular situation.

Setup a system for receiving payments for your podcast

To set up a system for receiving payments for your podcast, you will need to choose a payment processor that is compatible with your needs and the preferences of your audience. Some popular options include PayPal, Stripe, and Square. Once you have chosen a payment processor, you will need to create an account and set up your payment preferences. This will typically involve providing your personal and financial information, as well as setting up your payment methods and account preferences. Once your account is set up, you can start accepting payments for your podcast.

To facilitate payments, you will need to provide a way for your audience to make payments, such as through a link on your website or a button on your podcast page. You can also use a platform like Patreon, which allows listeners to support their favorite creators by making recurring payments. Patreon makes it easy to manage your supporters and offers exclusive content or perks in exchange for their support.

It's important to remember that different payment processors may have different fees and restrictions, so it's important to do your research and choose the option that is right for you. You should also make sure to comply with any relevant laws and regulations regarding online payments and financial transactions.

What is the importance of building a loyal audience?

Building a loyal podcast audience is important for a number of reasons. Firstly, a loyal audience can provide you with a consistent and dedicated group of listeners who are invested in your content and are more likely to support you through monetization efforts. This can help to ensure the success and sustainability of your podcast.

Secondly, a loyal audience can provide valuable feedback and insights that can help you improve your content and grow your show. By engaging with your audience and soliciting their feedback, you can learn what they like and don't like about your show and use that information to make improvements and continue to grow.

Thirdly, a loyal audience can also help to increase the visibility and reach of your podcast. By sharing your content with their friends and followers, your audience can help to spread the word about your show and attract new listeners. This can help to increase your audience size and ultimately drive more revenue for your podcast.

There are several ways that a podcaster can build a loyal audience, including:

1. **Create high-quality content:** Providing valuable and engaging content is essential for building a loyal audience. By consistently delivering content that is interesting, informative, and entertaining, you can attract and retain listeners who are interested in your show.

2. **Engage with your audience:** Building a loyal audience is not a one-way street. You need to actively engage with your listeners in order to build a relationship with them and foster a sense of community. This can involve responding to comments and messages, soliciting feedback, and interacting with your audience on social media.

3. **Offer exclusive content or perks:** One way to build a loyal audience is by offering exclusive content or perks that are only

available to your most dedicated listeners. This could include bonus episodes, behind-the-scenes content, or access to special events or merchandise. By providing these perks, you can incentivize your audience to support you and become more invested in your success.

4. **Consistency:** Consistency is also important for building a loyal audience. By releasing new episodes on a regular schedule, you can help your audience to know what to expect and when to tune in. This can help to build anticipation and create a sense of loyalty among your listeners.

Building a loyal audience requires effort and dedication, but the rewards can be well worth it. By providing valuable content, engaging with your audience, and offering exclusive perks, you can foster a sense of community and create a dedicated group of supporters who are invested in your success. By engaging with your audience and providing them with valuable content, you can foster a sense of community and create a dedicated group of supporters who are invested in your success.

Profit from your podcast without making money

While monetizing your podcast is a common way to generate income, it's not the only way to profit from your show. In fact, there are many ways to profit from your podcast without making actual money. Some examples include:

1. **Building your brand:** By creating a successful podcast, you can increase your visibility and establish yourself as an expert in your field. This can lead to opportunities for speaking engagements, consulting work, or other forms of income.

2. **Promoting your business:** If you have a business or product, a podcast can be a powerful marketing tool. By providing

valuable content and engaging with your audience, you can promote your business and attract new customers.

3. **Networking:** Podcasting can also be a great way to make connections and build relationships with other experts in your field. By interviewing guests or collaborating with other podcasters, you can expand your network and potentially open up new opportunities for yourself.

4. **Personal growth:** Finally, creating a successful podcast can also be personally rewarding. By sharing your ideas and stories with a wider audience, you can help to inspire and educate others, which can be deeply fulfilling.

There are many ways to profit from your podcast beyond making actual money. By focusing on building your brand, promoting your business, networking, and personal growth, you can create a successful and rewarding podcasting venture.

Conclusion

Monetizing your podcast can be a great way to turn your passion into a profitable venture. By exploring the various ways to generate income from your show, including advertising, sponsorships, and selling merchandise, you can determine the best approach for your particular situation. Building a loyal audience and creating high-quality content are also essential for maximizing your income potential and ensuring the success of your podcast. By following the strategies outlined in this chapter, you can take the first steps toward monetizing your podcast and achieving financial success.

Key Points:

Considerations for Monetization: In order to monetize your podcast effectively, it is important to assess your goals and circumstances. Take the time to determine if monetization is necessary for you. If your aim is to make a living from your podcast or utilize it as a promotional tool for your business, then monetizing becomes crucial. By monetizing your podcast, you can gain the resources and financial support needed to invest in your show, ultimately turning your passion into a profitable venture.

Strategies for Monetizing: When it comes to monetizing your podcast, there are various strategies available to you. These include advertising, sponsorships, crowdfunding, merchandise sales, courses/workshops, and consulting/coaching. Explore these different methods and select the ones that best align with your audience and content. It may require some experimentation to find the most suitable approach for your specific situation. By adopting effective monetization strategies, you can generate income from your podcast and unlock its full potential.

Building a Loyal Audience: Building a loyal audience is a critical aspect of podcast monetization. To achieve this, focus on providing high-quality content that attracts and retains listeners. Engage with your audience by offering exclusive perks and actively interacting with them through comments, messages, and social media. Consistency in releasing episodes is also key. By building a loyal audience, you increase the visibility and reach of your podcast, leading to more revenue opportunities. This dedicated group of supporters will provide you with consistent support and valuable feedback, helping you refine your content and drive the success of your podcast.

Chapter 7: Growing Your Podcast Audience & Building Your Brand

With millions of people tuning in to listen to their favorite shows daily, starting a podcast has become an increasingly attractive option for individuals and businesses looking to share their ideas, stories, and expertise with a wide audience.

But simply creating a podcast isn't enough to ensure success. To truly thrive in the world of podcasting, you need to be strategic about growing your audience and building your brand. In this chapter, we'll discuss some key strategies for doing just that.

We'll start by discussing the importance of having a clear and compelling concept for your podcast, and how to effectively communicate that concept to potential listeners. We'll also talk about the role of networking and collaborations in growing your audience, and how to use social media and other online platforms to promote your podcast and connect with your listeners.

Finally, we'll explore the various ways you can use your podcast to build your personal or business brand, and how to leverage your growing audience to achieve your goals and drive success. Whether you're just starting out or looking to take your podcast to the next level, this chapter will provide valuable insights and practical advice for growing your podcast audience and building your brand.

There are several benefits of having a successful podcast. Some of the most notable benefits include:

1. **Increased exposure:** A successful podcast can reach a wider audience and gain more visibility, which can lead to more opportunities for collaboration, partnerships, and sponsorships.

2. **Revenue opportunities:** A successful podcast can generate revenue through advertising, sponsorships, and other forms of monetization. This can provide a valuable source of income for the creators of the podcast.

3. **Community building:** A successful podcast can foster a dedicated community of listeners who engage with the content and provide valuable feedback and insights. This can help to build a loyal and engaged audience for the podcast.

4. **Influence and impact:** A successful podcast can establish its creators as influential figures in their niche or industry, which can lead to opportunities for speaking engagements, consulting, or other forms of thought leadership.

Identifying Your Target Audience

Knowing who your podcast is intended for is important for several reasons. First, it can help you to create content that is relevant and engaging to your target audience. By understanding the interests, needs, and preferences of your intended audience, you can create episodes that are tailored to their interests and likely to resonate with them. This can help to increase the appeal and value of your podcast to your target audience.

Second, knowing who your podcast is intended for can also help you to effectively promote and market your podcast. By understanding the demographics, interests, and behaviors of your target audience, you can develop targeted and effective marketing strategies that are likely to reach and engage your intended audience. This can help to increase the visibility and success of your podcast.

Knowing who your podcast is intended for is crucial for creating content that resonates with your audience, promoting your podcast effectively, and ultimately growing your audience and building your brand.

There are several tips that can help you to identify and define your target podcast audience. Some of these tips include:

1. **Conduct market research:** Conducting market research can provide valuable insights into the demographics, interests, and behaviors of potential listeners for your podcast. This can help you to better understand your target audience and develop content and marketing strategies that are tailored to their interests and needs.

2. **Analyze your existing audience:** If you already have an audience for your podcast, analyzing their demographics and engagement can provide valuable insights into who your target audience is and what they are interested in. This can help you to create content and marketing strategies that are likely to resonate with your existing audience and attract more listeners like them.

3. **Identify your niche or topic:** Identifying your niche or topic can also help you to define your target audience. For example, if your podcast covers a specific topic or industry, you can target listeners who are interested in that topic or industry. This can help you to create content that is relevant and valuable to your target audience.

These tips can help you to identify and define your target podcast audience, which can enable you to create content and marketing strategies that are tailored to their interests and needs.

Developing a Strong Brand Identity

A strong podcast brand can provide several benefits for your podcast. Some of the most notable benefits include:

1. **Increased visibility and recognition:** A strong podcast brand can make your podcast more visible and recognizable to potential listeners. This can help to differentiate your podcast from competitors and make it more memorable to potential listeners.

2. **Enhanced credibility and trust:** A strong podcast brand can also enhance the credibility and trust of your podcast in the eyes of potential listeners. By creating a professional and consistent brand, you can establish your podcast as a trusted and reputable source of information or entertainment.

3. **Improved engagement and loyalty:** A strong podcast brand can also improve engagement and loyalty among your existing audience. By creating a consistent and cohesive brand identity, you can foster a sense of community and belong among your listeners, which can lead to increased engagement and loyalty.

4. **More opportunities for growth and monetization:** A strong podcast brand can also provide more opportunities for growth and monetization. By establishing your podcast as a trusted and influential platform, you can attract more listeners and generate more revenue through advertising, sponsorships, and other forms of monetization.

A podcaster can create a consistent and cohesive brand identity for their podcast by following these steps:

1. **Define your brand values and positioning:** Start by defining the core values and positioning of your podcast. This can include your unique value proposition, target audience, and target market. This will provide a foundation for all of your branding efforts.

2. **Develop a unique and memorable name:** Choose a unique and memorable name for your podcast that captures the essence of your brand and resonates with your target audience. This can help to differentiate your podcast from competitors and make it more recognizable to potential listeners.

3. **Create a consistent and cohesive visual identity:** Develop a consistent and cohesive visual identity for your podcast, including a logo, color palette, and font. This can help to create a professional and recognizable brand for your podcast.

4. **Engage with your audience:** Engage with your audience through social media, email newsletters, and other channels to build a community of loyal listeners and foster a strong brand for your podcast.

You can create a consistent and cohesive brand identity for your podcast that is unique, memorable, and professional. This can help to differentiate your podcast from competitors and attract more listeners.

Creating Engaging and High-Quality Content

The importance of producing engaging and high-quality content for your podcast cannot be overstated. Engaging and high-quality content is crucial for attracting and retaining listeners, building a loyal and engaged audience, and ultimately achieving success for your podcast.

Producing engaging content means creating episodes that are interesting, informative, entertaining, or otherwise compelling to your target audience. This can help to keep your listeners engaged and coming back for more episodes. It can also help to establish your podcast as a valuable and trusted source of information or entertainment in your niche or industry.

Producing high-quality content means creating episodes that are well-researched, well-written, well-produced, and free of technical errors or other distractions. This can help to enhance the credibility and professionalism of your podcast and make it more appealing to potential listeners. It can also help to improve the overall listening experience for your audience, which can foster a sense of trust and loyalty.

Overall, producing engaging and high-quality content is essential for attracting and retaining listeners, building a loyal and engaged audience, and achieving success for your podcast.

Here are some tips for developing a compelling format, engaging with your audience, and delivering consistently strong podcast episodes:

1. **Develop a compelling format:** Develop a format for your podcast that is engaging, informative, entertaining, or otherwise compelling to your target audience. This can include the length of your episodes, the frequency of your episodes, and the structure and format of your content.

2. **Engage with your audience:** Engage with your audience through social media, email newsletters, and other channels to build a community of loyal listeners and foster a strong brand for your podcast. This can include responding to comments and questions, soliciting feedback, and promoting new episodes.

3. **Deliver consistently strong episodes:** Consistently produce high-quality, engaging, and well-researched episodes for your podcast. This can help to establish your podcast as a trusted and reputable source of information or entertainment in your niche or industry.

4. **Continuously improve and evolve:** Continuously seek feedback from your audience and analyze data on your listenership to identify opportunities for improvement and evolution. This can help you to continuously improve and evolve your podcast to better serve your audience and achieve success.

By following these tips, you can develop a compelling format, engage with your audience, and deliver consistently strong episodes for your podcast. This can help to attract and retain listeners, build a loyal and engaged audience, and achieve success for your podcast.

Promoting Your Podcast and Building Your Audience

Marketing and promotion play a critical role in growing your podcast audience. Marketing is the process of creating awareness and interest in your podcast among potential listeners, while promotion is the process of encouraging those potential listeners to take action and become regular listeners.

Effective marketing and promotion can help to increase the visibility and recognition of your podcast among potential listeners. This can include leveraging social media, email marketing, and other channels to reach and engage with potential listeners. It can also include collaborating with other creators and influencers to increase the exposure of your podcast to new audiences.

Effective marketing and promotion can also help to differentiate your podcast from competitors and position it as a unique and valuable source of information or entertainment in your niche or industry. This can help to attract more potential listeners and convert them into regular listeners.

Marketing and promotion are crucial for growing your podcast audience. By effectively leveraging marketing and promotion strategies, you can increase the visibility and recognition of your podcast, differentiate it from competitors, and attract more regular listeners.

Here are some tips to help you effectively promote your podcast to potential listeners and grow your audience:

1. **Leverage social media:** Use social media platforms, such as Twitter, Facebook, and Instagram, to promote your podcast to potential listeners. This can include sharing links to your episodes, engaging with your audience, and collaborating with other creators and influencers.

2. **Use email marketing:** Use email marketing to promote your podcast to your existing audience and to potential listeners who have subscribed to your email list. This can include sending regular newsletters with updates on new episodes and other relevant information.

3. **Collaborate with other creators and influencers:** Collaborate with other creators and influencers in your niche or industry to promote your podcast to their audiences. This can include guest appearances on other podcasts, cross-promotion, and co-branded content.

4. **Optimize your podcast for search:** Optimize your podcast for search by using keywords in your episode titles, descriptions, and metadata. This can help to improve the visibility of your podcast in search engine results, which can attract more potential listeners.

5. **Utilize paid advertising:** Consider using paid advertising, such as Google AdWords or Facebook Ads, to promote your podcast to targeted audiences. This can help to increase the visibility and recognition of your podcast among potential listeners.

6. **Utilize guest appearances:** Consider appearing as a guest on other podcasts or media outlets to promote your podcast to new audiences. This can help to increase the exposure of your podcast to potential listeners and establish you as an expert or thought leader in your niche or industry.

7. **Engage with your audience:** Engage with your audience through social media, email newsletters, and other channels to build a community of loyal listeners and foster a strong brand for your podcast. This can include responding to comments and questions, soliciting feedback, and promoting new episodes.

Conclusion

In this chapter, we discussed the importance of building a strong brand and growing an audience for your podcast. A strong brand and growing audience can provide numerous benefits, such as increased exposure, revenue opportunities, and the ability to establish influence and impact in your niche or industry.

The chapter has also provided tips for identifying and defining your target audience, developing a strong brand identity, creating engaging and high-quality content, promoting your podcast, and monetizing your audience. By following these tips, you can effectively grow your podcast audience and build a strong brand for your podcast.

The rewards of growing your podcast audience and building a strong brand are numerous and can provide valuable opportunities for exposure, revenue, influence, and impact. However, the process of growing your podcast audience and building your brand is ongoing and requires continuous effort and improvement. By consistently producing engaging and high-quality content, promoting your podcast effectively, and monetizing your audience, you can continue to grow your podcast audience and build a successful and influential brand.

Chapter 8: Troubleshooting Common Podcasting Challenges

We know that podcasting has become a popular medium for sharing ideas, stories, and information with a wide audience. However, even with the best planning and preparation, podcasting can come with its own set of challenges. In this chapter, we will explore some of the most common problems that podcasters face and provide solutions for troubleshooting them. Whether you are just starting out with podcasting or are an experienced pro, this chapter will provide valuable insights and tips for overcoming common obstacles and ensuring a successful recording.

Problem #1 - Poor audio quality: This can be caused by a variety of factors, such as background noise, poor microphone technique, or insufficient recording equipment.

Solution: One solution to poor audio quality is to use a high-quality microphone and recording equipment, and to minimize background noise during recording.

Problem #2 - Audio distortion or feedback: This can occur when the audio signal is too loud or when there is a problem with the recording equipment.

Solution: One solution to audio distortion or feedback is to adjust the volume levels during recording, and to check and troubleshoot the equipment for any issues.

Problem #3: Problems with recording equipment: This can include malfunctioning microphones, faulty cables or connections, or issues with software or recording devices.

Solution: One solution to problems with recording equipment is to regularly maintain and check the equipment for any issues, and to troubleshoot or repair any malfunctioning components.

Problem #4: Difficulties with editing and post-production: This can include challenges with editing audio files, adding music or sound effects, and preparing episodes for publishing.

Solution: One solution to difficulties with editing and post-production is to use specialized software and tools for editing audio files, and to seek advice and guidance from more experienced podcasters or professionals.

Problem #5: Issues with uploading and publishing episodes: This can include problems with publishing to podcast hosting platforms or issues with sharing episodes on listening platforms.

Solution: One solution to issues with uploading and publishing episodes is to carefully follow the guidelines and instructions provided by podcast hosting platforms, and to troubleshoot any technical problems with the help of customer support or online resources.

Problem #6: Issues with uploading and publishing episodes: This can include problems with publishing to podcast hosting platforms or issues with sharing episodes on listening platforms.

Solution: One solution to problems with website and podcast hosting platforms is to choose a reputable and reliable provider, and to seek advice and support from their customer service team if any issues arise.

Problem #7: Difficulties with formatting and sharing episodes:
This can include problems with ensuring that episodes are properly formatted for different listening platforms, as well as challenges with promoting and sharing episodes on social media and other online channels.

Solution: One solution to difficulties with formatting and sharing episodes is to carefully research and follow the guidelines provided by different listening platforms, and to use social media and other online channels to promote and share episodes.

Dealing with negative feedback and haters

As a podcaster, it is inevitable that you will receive some negative feedback and criticism from listeners. While it can be difficult to hear negative comments about your work, it is important to remember that not everyone will agree with you or like your content. It is also important to distinguish between constructive criticism, which can help you improve and grow as a podcaster, and destructive or malicious comments, which are often intended to hurt or offend you.

One way to deal with negative feedback and haters is to try to remain calm and professional. Don't let your emotions get the better of you, and avoid getting into a heated argument or engaging with trolls. Instead, take a step back and try to see the situation from the other person's perspective. Consider whether there is any truth to their comments and whether there are any changes or improvements that you can make to your content.

Another way to deal with negative feedback and haters is to engage with your audience and listen to their concerns and suggestions. Respond to their comments and questions in a polite and respectful manner, and show that you are open to feedback and willing to improve. This can help to build trust and credibility with your listeners, and can also provide valuable insights and ideas for future episodes.

Finally, remember that not everyone will like your podcast, and that's okay. Focus on creating content that resonates with your target audience, and don't be discouraged by the occasional negative comment or criticism. With time, you will develop a loyal and engaged audience who appreciate and support your work.

Here are some tips for dealing with negative feedback:

1. **Remain calm and professional:** It can be difficult to hear negative comments about your work, but it is important to stay calm and avoid getting into a heated argument or engaging with trolls.

2. **Consider the other person's perspective:** Try to see the situation from the other person's perspective, and consider whether there is any truth to their comments.

3. **Engage with your audience:** Respond to negative feedback in a polite and respectful manner, and show that you are open to feedback and willing to improve.

4. **Don't take it personally:** Remember that not everyone will like your podcast, and that's okay. Focus on creating content that resonates with your target audience.

5. **Use negative feedback as a learning opportunity:** Use negative feedback as a way to improve and grow as a podcaster, and seek out constructive criticism from trusted sources.

6. **Ignore trolls and haters:** Don't waste your time and energy on people who are intentionally trying to hurt or offend you. Ignore them and move on.

7. **Keep creating:** Don't let negative feedback discourage you from continuing to create and share your podcast. Keep producing content that you are passionate about, and trust that your audience will appreciate it.

Staying motivated and consistent with your podcasting schedule

There are several ways that a podcaster can stay motivated to create their podcast. Some of these include setting specific and achievable goals, planning and organizing the podcast in advance, involving others in the process, and taking breaks when needed. Additionally, a podcaster can stay motivated by regularly reviewing and celebrating their achievements, seeking feedback and support from others, and by finding ways to stay engaged and excited about their podcast topic. It is also important to remember that motivation can come from within and that a strong passion and commitment to the podcast can help to keep the fire burning, even when challenges arise.

To stay consistent with their podcast, a podcaster can follow a regular publishing schedule and stick to it as much as possible. This can help to build a sense of expectation and anticipation among listeners, and can also make it easier for the podcaster to plan and prepare episodes in advance. It is also important to be consistent in the quality and content of the podcast, as this can help to maintain the trust and loyalty of the audience.

Another way to stay consistent is to use a dedicated recording and editing setup and to stick to a consistent workflow for producing episodes. This can help to minimize distractions and interruptions, and can also ensure that episodes are produced to a high standard. Consistency in the podcast's branding and presentation can also help to establish the podcast's identity and credibility and can make it easier for listeners to recognize and engage with the podcast.

Finally, it is important to remember that consistency does not mean perfection. It is okay to make mistakes or to experiment with different formats or topics, as long as the podcast remains true to its core values and mission. Consistency is about maintaining a steady and reliable presence, and about continuing to create and share valuable and engaging content, even when challenges arise.

Conclusion

Podcasting can come with its own set of challenges, from technical issues to negative feedback and criticism. However, with the right knowledge and tools, these challenges can be overcome and turned into opportunities for growth and improvement. This chapter has provided valuable insights and tips for troubleshooting common podcasting challenges and has shown that with dedication and perseverance, it is possible to create and maintain a successful and engaging podcast. Whether you are a beginner or an experienced pro, these tips and strategies can help you overcome obstacles and ensure that your podcast reaches its full potential.

Chapter 9: Conclusions, Recaps, and Next Steps

Podcasting is a popular and rewarding medium for sharing ideas, stories, and information with a wide audience. By following the steps outlined in this book, you can successfully launch and grow your own podcast.

Key points covered in the book

- In the first chapter, we introduced the basics of podcasting and discussed the various formats and topics that are popular among podcast listeners. In the second chapter, we explored how to choose a topic and format that will be engaging and relevant to your target audience.

- The second chapter covers choosing a topic and format for your podcast. This includes considering the interests of your target audience, as well as the strengths and expertise of the podcast host. The chapter also discusses the various podcast formats, such as solo, co-hosted, panel, and interview style, and how to choose the best one for your content.

- In the third chapter, we covered the importance of planning and preparing for your podcast, including setting goals, creating a schedule, and gathering the necessary equipment and resources. In the fourth chapter, we discussed the process of recording and editing your podcast, including tips for achieving high-quality audio and editing software recommendations.

- The fourth chapter covers the process of recording and editing your podcast. This includes tips for achieving high-quality audio, as well as recommendations for editing software and other resources. The chapter also discusses the importance of following a consistent recording and editing process to ensure that each episode is polished and professional.

- In the fifth chapter, we explored the various ways you can promote and distribute your podcast, including submitting to popular directories and using social media to reach new listeners. In the sixth chapter, we discussed the potential for monetizing your podcast through advertising, sponsorships, and other revenue streams.

- The sixth chapter discusses the potential for monetizing your podcast through advertising, sponsorships, and other revenue streams. This includes advice on working with advertisers and sponsors, as well as tips for maximizing your earnings potential. The chapter also covers the legal and ethical considerations of monetizing your podcast, and how to avoid alienating your audience.

- In the seventh chapter, we covered strategies for growing your podcast audience and building your brand, including engaging with your listeners and collaborating with other podcasters. Finally, in the eighth chapter, we discussed some common challenges that podcasters face and provide troubleshooting tips for overcoming them.

- The eighth chapter covers common challenges that podcasters face and provides troubleshooting tips for overcoming them. This includes advice on dealing with difficult guests, technical issues, and low audience engagement. The chapter also discusses strategies for staying motivated and committed to your podcast, even when faced with obstacles and setbacks.

Set goals and create a plan for continuing to grow and improve your podcast

1. **Define your goals and objectives** for the podcast, such as increasing the number of listeners, improving the quality of the content, or generating revenue.

2. **Identify your target audience** and what they want from the podcast, and create content that is relevant and engaging to that audience.

3. **Develop a schedule** for recording and releasing episodes, and stick to it consistently to maintain momentum and build an audience.

4. **Invest in high-quality equipment and editing software** to improve the sound and production value of the podcast.

5. **Promote the podcast** through social media, advertising, and other channels to reach new listeners and grow the audience.

6. **Engage with the audience** and solicit feedback to understand what they like and don't like about the podcast, and use that information to improve and evolve the content.

7. **Seek collaborations** and partnerships with other podcasters and industry experts to add value and credibility to the podcast.

8. **Continuously evaluate the progress** of the podcast and make adjustments to the content, format, and promotion strategy as needed to achieve the desired results.

Next steps in your podcast journey

Now that you've read this book, the logical next steps for a podcaster would be to:

- **Choose a topic and format** for your podcast that will be engaging and relevant to your target audience.

- **Plan and prepare** for your podcast, including setting goals, creating a schedule, and gathering the necessary equipment and resources.

- **Record and edit** your podcast, following a consistent process and using high-quality equipment and editing software.

- **Promote and distribute** your podcast by submitting it to popular directories and using social media to reach new listeners.

- **Consider monetizing your podcast** through advertising, sponsorships, or other revenue streams, while maintaining legal and ethical standards and avoiding alienating your audience.

- **Grow your podcast audience** and build your brand by engaging with your listeners and collaborating with other podcasters.

- **Troubleshoot common challenges and obstacles**, such as technical issues and low audience engagement, and stay motivated and committed to your podcast.

There are many resources and support available for ongoing learning and development in podcasting. These can include:

- **Podcasting forums and communities**, where experienced podcasters share their knowledge and provide support and advice to newcomers. These forums can be a great way to learn about the latest trends and techniques in podcasting, as well as connect with other podcasters and potential collaborators.

- **Podcasting conferences and workshops**, where experts and professionals in the field share their insights and experiences. These events can provide valuable learning opportunities, as well as networking opportunities with other podcasters and industry professionals.

- **Podcasting courses and online training programs**, provide step-by-step guidance on how to start and grow a successful podcast. These courses can be a great way to learn the technical and creative skills needed to produce high-quality audio content, as well as the business and marketing strategies needed to promote and monetize your podcast.

- **Podcasting books and guides**, provide in-depth information and advice on all aspects of podcasting, from choosing a topic and format to recording and editing, promoting and distributing, and monetizing your podcast. These books can be a great resource for both beginners and experienced podcasters looking to improve their skills and knowledge.

There are many resources and support available for ongoing learning and development in podcasting. By taking advantage of these resources, you can continue to improve and grow your podcast, and connect with other like-minded individuals in the podcasting community.

Podcasting is a rewarding and engaging medium that allows you to share your ideas and experiences with a wide audience. By following the steps outlined in this book, you can successfully launch and grow your own podcast.

Scan this QR code for all my podcasting resources: